# Guide to Alpine

## Practical Guide

A. De Quattro

Copyright © 2024

Practical Guide

# 1. Introduction to Alpine.js

Alpine.js is a lightweight JavaScript framework designed to provide reactive and dynamic functionality within web pages with a minimalist and simplicity-oriented approach. In recent years, with the evolution of web development, various libraries and frameworks have emerged to enhance web page interactivity. However, many of these require complex configurations and a steeper learning curve. Alpine.js serves as an alternative to these heavier frameworks, offering a lightweight and fast solution for creating dynamic user interfaces. In this article, we'll explore what Alpine.js is, why it might be the right choice for your project, how to install it, and how it compares to other popular JavaScript libraries such as Vue.js, React, and jQuery.

#### What is Alpine.js?

Alpine.js is a JavaScript library designed for

developers who want to add interactivity to their web pages without having to load heavy or complex frameworks. It aims to provide a reactive and declarative approach to web development, allowing you to manage states, events, and logic directly within the HTML markup.

#### History and Philosophy

Alpine.js was created by Caleb Porzio, with the first version released in 2019. The philosophy behind the library is to offer a minimalist solution that sits between the simple DOM manipulations of jQuery and the complexity of more robust frameworks like Vue.js or React. In this sense, Alpine.js positions itself as a "toolbox" for developers who want to implement complex logic but prefer not to adopt solutions that require configuration files, build tools, or elaborate project structures.

#### Key Features

- **Simplicity**: Alpine.js allows you to add reactive JavaScript functionality directly in the HTML code, similar to Vue.js, but with reduced syntax and minimal configuration.

- **Lightweight**: One of Alpine.js's strengths is its extremely small size. The minified version weighs only a few kilobytes, making it ideal for projects where load time is crucial.

- **Reactivity**: Alpine.js is reactive by nature, meaning that changes in the application state are immediately reflected in the DOM without manual intervention. This makes development very smooth.

- **Use of Directives**: Similar to Vue.js, Alpine.js uses directives within HTML markup to define reactive behaviors. For example, directives like `x-data` to define application data or `x-show` to control element visibility.

- **Compatibility**: Being purely JavaScript-based, Alpine.js is compatible with most other front-end frameworks or libraries and can be easily integrated into existing projects.

- **No Configuration Needed**: There is no need to configure build tools or set up complex environments. Alpine.js is a simple JavaScript file that can be included in any web page via a `<script>` tag.

#### Why Choose Alpine.js?

There are several reasons why you might choose Alpine.js over other more complex JavaScript solutions:

1. **Lightweight**:

    If your goal is to keep a web page light and fast, Alpine.js is an excellent choice. Unlike React or Vue.js, which often require heavier infrastructure, Alpine.js has a minimal impact on page weight. This is particularly important in scenarios where performance is crucial, such as mobile-first projects or sites with a large audience that may have slow internet connections.

2. **Simplicity of Integration**:

With Alpine.js, there's no need to preconfigure tools like Webpack, Babel, or Node.js. You can start using it immediately by adding a single `<script>` tag to your page. This makes it perfect for smaller projects or prototypes where you need a quick solution without complex configurations.

3. **Power Without Complexity**:

Despite its simplicity, Alpine.js is not limited. With a clean and easy-to-learn syntax, Alpine.js allows you to create reactive user interfaces with advanced features such as state management, DOM manipulation, and two-way binding—characteristics typically found in more complex frameworks.

4. **Declarative Workflow**:

   Alpine.js follows a declarative approach similar to Vue.js. This means you can write your application's logic directly in the HTML markup, making the code more readable and maintainable. This approach makes Alpine.js ideal for projects where you want to avoid the traditional separation of HTML and JavaScript, favoring instead a tight integration of logic and presentation.

5. **Compatibility with Other Frameworks**:

   Since Alpine.js is a standalone library and doesn't require any external dependencies, it integrates easily with other technologies. For example, you can use Alpine.js alongside Laravel, Blade, or even larger frameworks like React and Vue without any conflicts.

6. **Growing Community**:

   Although Alpine.js is a relatively young library, its community is rapidly growing. There are already numerous resources, tutorials, and pre-built components available that can be used to extend the functionality of your application.

#### Installing Alpine.js

One of Alpine.js's main advantages is its ease of installation. No complex build processes, third-party dependencies, or sophisticated development tools are needed. Here are some methods to include Alpine.js in your projects:

1. **Including Alpine.js via CDN**:

The simplest way to use Alpine.js is to include it directly in your HTML page via a CDN (Content Delivery Network). This approach is ideal for lightweight projects and quick prototypes.

Here's how to do it:

```html
```

```html
<!DOCTYPE html>
<html lang="en">
<head>
    <meta charset="UTF-8">
    <meta name="viewport" content="width=device-width, initial-scale=1.0">
    <title>Alpine.js Example</title>
    <!-- Include Alpine.js -->
    <script defer src="https://cdn.jsdelivr.net/npm/alpinejs@3.x.x/dist/cdn.min.js"></script>
</head>
<body>
    <div x-data="{ message: 'Hello, Alpine!' }">
        <h1 x-text="message"></h1>
    </div>
</body>
</html>
```

```

In this example, the `<script>` tag includes Alpine.js directly from the jsDelivr CDN. The code inside the `<div>` uses the `x-data` directive to define a JavaScript object containing the application's data and the `x-text` directive to dynamically update the text of the `<h1>` element.

2. **Installation via NPM**:

If you're working on a project that uses a package manager like NPM (Node Package Manager), you can install Alpine.js as a dependency.

Here's how to do it:

Run the following command to install Alpine.js:
```

```bash
npm install alpinejs
```

After installing Alpine.js, you can import it into your main JavaScript file:

```javascript
import Alpine from 'alpinejs'

window.Alpine = Alpine

Alpine.start()
```

This approach is more suited for projects requiring build configuration, such as those using Webpack or Parcel. It is useful if you need more control over the library version or if you are integrating Alpine.js into a larger project with other dependencies.

#### Comparing with Other JavaScript Libraries

Alpine.js is often compared to larger, well-established JavaScript frameworks like Vue.js, React, and jQuery, as it sits between simple DOM manipulation and complex reactivity. Let's look at a detailed comparison with some of the most popular libraries.

**Alpine.js vs Vue.js**:

- **Size and Complexity**: Vue.js is much heavier than Alpine.js and requires more elaborate configuration. While Vue.js offers a range of advanced tools like routing and state management (with Vue Router and Vuex), Alpine.js focuses solely on the essential aspects of reactivity.

- **Learning Curve**: Alpine.js is easier for beginners to learn due to its simplified syntax and absence of complex tools like CLI and build configurations.

- **Ecosystem**: Vue.js has a much more developed and robust ecosystem, with support for creating SPA (Single Page Applications). Alpine.js is better suited for adding interactivity to static pages or projects that don't require the full stack of Vue.js features.

**Alpine.js vs React**:

- **Architecture**: React is based on a component-based approach and uses JSX, a syntax extension that allows writing HTML markup within JavaScript. This requires more complex configuration and tools like Babel for code compilation.

- **Weight**: React is much heavier than Alpine.js. The base React library, without additional routing or state management tools, already has a significantly larger size compared to Alpine.js.

- **Usage**: React is ideal for large web applications that require complex state and rendering management. Alpine.js, on the other hand, is perfect for smaller projects or for those who need to add reactive features without setting up an entire infrastructure.

**Alpine.js vs jQuery**:

- **Modernity**: Alpine.js uses a more modern and reactive approach compared to jQuery, which relies on imperative DOM manipulation.

- **Weight**: Although jQuery is considered "lightweight," Alpine.js is even smaller and, due to its declarative approach, allows writing less code to achieve the same results.

- **Reactivity**: Alpine.js has built-in

reactive state management, while jQuery requires manual manipulation of events and states.

Alpine.js is a powerful and lightweight JavaScript library designed for developers looking to add interactivity to their web pages without the complexity of larger frameworks. With its simple syntax, reactive approach, and compatibility with other tools, Alpine.js represents an excellent choice for many projects.

## 2. Getting Started with Alpine.js

Alpine.js is a lightweight JavaScript library that allows you to add interactivity to a webpage in a simple and responsive way, without the complexity of heavier frameworks like React or Vue.js. Its ease of integration makes it ideal for projects that don't require large infrastructures but still need basic DOM manipulation and reactive logic. In this guide, we will explore how to start using Alpine.js, covering installation, configuration, project structure, and how to include the library in a website.

### Installing and Configuring Alpine.js

One of the main advantages of Alpine.js is its ease of use. There's no need to configure build tools like Webpack or set up a complex JavaScript environment. There are two primary ways to install Alpine.js:

1. **Via CDN** (Content Delivery Network)

2. **Via NPM** (Node Package Manager) for projects that require a more advanced build process

Let's look at both methods in detail.

#### Installation via CDN

The quickest way to start using Alpine.js is by including it directly in your webpage via a CDN. This approach is ideal for static websites or small projects that do not need an advanced development environment.

1. **Create a simple HTML file**: Suppose you're creating a basic HTML file. To include Alpine.js, simply add the `<script>` tag inside the HTML file.

```html
```

```html
<!DOCTYPE html>
<html lang="en">
<head>
  <meta charset="UTF-8">
  <meta name="viewport" content="width=device-width, initial-scale=1.0">
  <title>First Project with Alpine.js</title>
  <!-- Include Alpine.js from the CDN -->
  <script defer src="https://cdn.jsdelivr.net/npm/alpinejs@3.x.x/dist/cdn.min.js"></script>
</head>
<body>


  <div x-data="{ counter: 0 }">
    <button @click="counter++">Increment</button>
    <p>Counter: <span x-text="counter"></span></p>
```

```
    </div>


</body>
</html>
```

In this example:

- The `x-data` directive defines a reactive object containing a `counter` variable.

- The `@click` attribute is used to increment the `counter` variable each time the button is clicked.

- The `x-text` directive updates the text content inside the span to reflect the value of the `counter` variable.

2. **Advantages of using CDN**:

   - **Easy integration**: No need for complex build tools.

- **Performance**: By using a CDN, the JavaScript file is loaded from optimized and globally distributed servers, improving load times.

- **Automatic updates**: You can easily update Alpine.js by changing the version in the `<script>` tag.

#### Installation via NPM

If you're developing a project using a Node.js environment with a build system like Webpack or Parcel, you can install Alpine.js via NPM. This approach is useful for medium to large-sized projects that require a more modular and complex structure.

1. **Start with a Node.js project**: If you don't already have a Node.js project set up, create a new folder and initialize it with `npm init`.

```bash
mkdir alpinejs-project
```

```
cd alpinejs-project

npm init -y
```

2. **Install Alpine.js via NPM**:

```bash
npm install alpinejs
```

3. **Configure the JavaScript file**: After installing Alpine.js, you can import it into your main JavaScript file.

```javascript
import Alpine from 'alpinejs'

window.Alpine = Alpine
```

```
Alpine.start()
```

4. **Integrate with the build system**: In a typical Webpack or Parcel project, this file will be included and bundled together with other JavaScript files. Ensure your build system is configured to generate a final JavaScript file that also includes Alpine.js.

```html
<!DOCTYPE html>
<html lang="en">
<head>
    <meta charset="UTF-8">
    <meta name="viewport" content="width=device-width, initial-scale=1.0">
    <title>Alpine.js with Webpack</title>
    <!-- Include the bundle generated by Webpack -->
```

```html
    <script defer src="/dist/bundle.js"></script>
</head>
<body>

    <div x-data="{ open: false }">
        <button @click="open = !open">Toggle</button>
        <p x-show="open">This is an example with Alpine.js and Webpack</p>
    </div>

</body>
</html>
```

By including Alpine.js in the build process, you can manage dependencies and modules in a more structured way.

#### Advantages of Installation via NPM

- **Modularity**: You can organize your code in a modular way and maintain a better project structure.

- **Version control**: You can easily manage dependency versions using the `package.json` file.

- **Compatibility with build tools**: If your project uses Webpack, Parcel, or other build tools, integration with NPM is essential.

### Project Structure with Alpine.js

Alpine.js is highly flexible when it comes to project structure. It doesn't impose any specific structure, making it ideal for projects of all sizes. However, there are some best practices to follow to organize your code clearly and maintainably.

#### 1. Simple Static Projects

For simple projects that don't use a build system, the project structure can be very minimal:

```
my-project/
│
├── index.html
├── styles.css
└── app.js
```

In this case, `index.html` would include Alpine.js via a CDN and contain the main application logic. `styles.css` would contain the styles, while `app.js` could hold custom JavaScript functions not directly related to Alpine.js.

#### 2. Modular Projects with NPM and Webpack

For more complex projects using build tools and requiring a more organized structure, the project folder might look like this:

```
my-project/
│
├── dist/
│   └── bundle.js
├── src/
│   ├── components/
│   │   └── dropdown.js
│   ├── styles/
│   │   └── main.css
│   └── index.js
├── index.html
```

└── package.json
```

In this example:

- The `dist/` folder contains the files generated by the build system (e.g., Webpack).

- The `src/` folder contains the project's source files, organized by components and styles.

- The `index.js` file holds the main code that initializes Alpine.js and imports other modules or components.

A project organized this way is better suited for large applications that may evolve over time.

### Including Alpine.js in Your Project

After choosing the most suitable installation
```

method (CDN or NPM), you can start integrating Alpine.js into your project. Alpine.js offers a set of directives that allow you to add reactive logic and interactivity directly into HTML markup.

#### 1. Defining Data with `x-data`

The `x-data` directive is the heart of Alpine.js. It allows you to define an object containing application data that can be directly manipulated in the HTML markup.

Example usage of `x-data`:

```html
<div x-data="{ message: 'Hello Alpine.js' }">
    <p x-text="message"></p>
</div>
```

In this example:

- `x-data="{ message: 'Hello Alpine.js' }"` defines a data object that contains the `message` variable.

- `x-text="message"` inserts the content of the `message` variable inside the paragraph.

#### 2. Events with `@click`, `@input`, etc.

Alpine.js supports event listeners with a simple syntax using directives like `@click`, `@input`, `@mouseover`, etc.

Example of handling a `click` event:

```html
<div x-data="{ count: 0 }">
    <button @click="count+
```

+">Increment</button>

    <p x-text="count"></p>
</div>
```

In this example, each time the button is clicked, the `count` variable is incremented, and the updated value is shown in the paragraph using `x-text`.

#### 3. Conditional Rendering with `x-show` and `x-if`

Alpine.js also provides directives to manage the conditional display of elements.

- **`x-show`**: Shows or hides an element based on a condition.

```html

```html
<div x-data="{ visible: true }">
    <button @click="visible = !visible">Toggle Visibility</button>
    <p x-show="visible">This paragraph is visible.</p>
</div>
```

In this case, the paragraph is shown or hidden based on the value of the `visible` variable.

- **`x-if`**: Similar to `x-show`, but the element is actually removed or added to the DOM.

```html
<div x-data="{ isLoggedIn: false }">
    <button @click="isLoggedIn = !isLoggedIn">
        Toggle Login
```

```
</button>

<p x-if="isLoggedIn">You are logged in!</p>

<p x-if="!isLoggedIn">You are not logged in!</p>
</div>
```

In this example, the element is completely removed from the DOM when the condition is not met.

#### 4. Loops with `x-for`

Alpine.js also allows you to loop through arrays or objects using `x-for`.

Here's an example:

```html
<div x-data="{ items: ['Apple', 'Banana', 'Orange'] }">
    <ul>
        <li x-for="item in items" x-text="item"></li>
    </ul>
</div>
```

Here, `x-for` is used to iterate through the `items` array, and each element is displayed in a `<li>` element.

---

Alpine.js represents a lightweight, powerful, and easy-to-use solution for adding interactivity to web pages without the complexity of heavier front-end frameworks.

Its simple syntax and ease of integration make it ideal for a wide range of projects, from small static sites to more complex applications. Whether you choose to install it via CDN for quick projects or integrate it into a modular environment with NPM, Alpine.js provides flexibility and power to build dynamic user interfaces with ease.

# 3. Fundamental Concepts of Alpine.js

Alpine.js is a minimalist JavaScript library that provides reactive functionality to enhance the interactivity of a webpage, similar to more complex frameworks like Vue.js or React, but without the configuration complexity. Its syntax is declarative and integrates directly into the HTML markup, allowing developers to build interactive applications without writing large amounts of JavaScript code.

In this detailed guide, we will explore the **fundamental concepts of Alpine.js**, **state declarations**, how its **reactivity** works, and the use of **data and properties** to create interactive and reactive applications.

### 1. Fundamental Concepts

#### 1.1. Directives

Alpine.js is based on directives that extend HTML markup to introduce reactive and interactive logic. Directives are specific attributes that start with the `x-` prefix, such as `x-data`, `x-bind`, `x-show`, and `x-for`.

Here are the main directives of Alpine.js:

- **x-data**: Defines the local data context within an element. This creates data reactivity for all nested elements.

- **x-bind**: Binds HTML properties to dynamic data.

- **x-show**: Shows or hides an element based on a boolean condition.

- **x-on**: Assigns an event handler (e.g., click, input).

- **x-text**: Inserts text content based on a dynamic value.

- **x-model**: Handles two-way binding between inputs and data.

Basic example of using these directives:

```html
<div x-data="{ count: 0 }">
    <button @click="count++">Increment</button>
    <p x-text="count"></p>
</div>
```

In this example, the `count` object is declared with `x-data` and updated via a `click` event (with `@click`). The value of `count` is dynamically displayed using `x-text`.

#### 1.2. Components

In Alpine.js, a component is simply an HTML block with a data context defined via the `x-data` directive. A component can contain logic, methods, and interactions with the DOM.

Example of an Alpine.js component:

```html
<div x-data="{ open: false }">
    <button @click="open = !open">Toggle Menu</button>
    <div x-show="open">
        <ul>
            <li>Option 1</li>
            <li>Option 2</li>
            <li>Option 3</li>
        </ul>
    </div>
</div>
```

In this case, the component manages a dropdown menu that is shown or hidden based on the `open` state.

#### 1.3. Declarative Reactivity

Alpine.js follows the paradigm of declarative reactivity, where changes in state are automatically reflected in the DOM, without the need to directly manipulate HTML elements. This philosophy makes the code more readable and easier to maintain.

### 2. State Declarations

#### 2.1. `x-data` - State Declaration

The `x-data` directive is the cornerstone of state management in Alpine.js. It allows you to define a data object within an HTML element, which Alpine.js observes for any changes.

Here's an example of using `x-data` to declare state:

```html
```

```
<div x-data="{ counter: 0, message: 'Welcome!' }">
    <button @click="counter++">Increment</button>
    <p x-text="message + ' You have clicked ' + counter + ' times.'"></p>
</div>
```

- `x-data="{ counter: 0, message: 'Welcome!' }"`: This declares a local state object with two properties, `counter` and `message`.

- Each time the button is clicked, the counter is incremented.

- The text displayed in the paragraph dynamically changes to reflect the updated `counter` value.

#### 2.2. Composite State and Complex Objects

In Alpine.js, the state can also consist of complex objects or arrays. Here's an example where we manage an array of objects:

```html
<div x-data="{ tasks: [{ id: 1, name: 'Buy milk', done: false }, { id: 2, name: 'Go jogging', done: false }] }">
    <ul>
        <li x-for="task in tasks" :key="task.id">
            <label>
                <input type="checkbox" x-model="task.done">
                <span x-bind:class="{ 'line-through': task.done }" x-text="task.name"></span>
            </label>
        </li>
    </ul>
</div>
```

```

In this example:

- We declare an array of objects as state with `x-data`.

- We use `x-for` to iterate over the array and generate `<li>` elements.

- We bind the checkbox to the `task.done` object using `x-model`, allowing us to update the state whenever the checkbox is checked.

- We use `x-bind:class` to conditionally apply a class (`line-through`) based on the `done` status of each task.

### 3. Alpine.js Reactivity

Alpine.js automatically handles the reactivity of HTML elements by synchronizing the DOM with the underlying data model. This means that any changes to the data declared
```

via `x-data` will be immediately reflected in the DOM.

#### 3.1. Concept of Reactivity

Reactivity in Alpine.js works by monitoring changes to the data and updating the DOM whenever the data changes. Unlike other libraries like Vue.js, which use a "virtual DOM," Alpine.js interacts directly with the real DOM, but efficiently by observing the declared data.

A more complex example of reactivity might be:

```html
<div x-data="{ temp: 20 }">
    <p>Temperature: <span x-text="temp"></span>°C</p>
    <button @click="temp++">Increase</button>
```

```
    <button @click="temp--">Decrease</button>
    <p x-bind:class="{ 'text-red-600': temp > 25, 'text-blue-600': temp < 15 }">
      The temperature is <span x-text="temp > 25 ? 'high' : (temp < 15 ? 'low' : 'normal')"></span>.
    </p>
  </div>
```

In this example:

- The `temp` variable represents the temperature and is incremented or decremented via buttons.

- The paragraph dynamically changes color depending on whether the temperature is high or low, using `x-bind:class`.

- The text in the paragraph changes based on the temperature using a ternary condition with `x-text`.

#### 3.2. Reactivity with Events

Alpine.js allows you to create reactive logic based on DOM events, such as `click`, `input`, `mouseover`, etc. Each event can trigger a state update, which Alpine.js handles automatically.

Here's an example with an input field that updates the state in real-time:

```html
<div x-data="{ name: '' }">
    <input type="text" x-model="name" placeholder="Enter your name">
    <p>Hello, <span x-text="name"></span>!</p>
</div>
```

In this example, the input is bound to the `name` property via `x-model`. Each time the user types into the field, the value of `name` changes, and the text displayed in the paragraph updates in real-time.

#### 3.3. Reactivity with `x-effect`

Alpine.js also introduces the concept of `x-effect`, which allows you to run a piece of code every time any of the declared data changes. This is useful for executing side effects or dynamically updating complex elements.

```html
<div x-data="{ width: window.innerWidth }" x-init="window.addEventListener('resize', () => width = window.innerWidth)">

  <p>The window width is: <span x-text="width"></span> pixels</p>

  <div x-effect="console.log('The width changed:', width)"></div>
</div>
```

```

In this example, we use `x-effect` to monitor changes to `width` and log a message to the console whenever it changes.

### 4. Using Data and Properties

#### 4.1. Dynamic Properties with `x-bind`

The `x-bind` directive allows you to dynamically bind HTML property values to component data. It can be used to bind any HTML attribute, such as classes, styles, IDs, or even custom attributes.

Here's an example of using `x-bind` to manage dynamic classes:

```html
<div x-data="{ active: false }">

```
    <button @click="active = !active" x-bind:class="{ 'bg-blue-500': active, 'bg-gray-500': !active }">
        Toggle Classes
    </button>
</div>
```

Here, the button's class dynamically changes based on the `active` state.

#### 4.2. Two-Way Binding with `x-model`

`x-model` is used for two-way binding between form elements (inputs, textareas, checkboxes, etc.) and component data. Whenever the user modifies the input, the associated data is automatically updated, and vice versa.

Example:

```html
<div x-data="{ message: 'Alpine.js' }">
    <input type="text" x-model="message">
    <p x-text="message"></p>
</div>
```

In this case, the input value and the paragraph text are bidirectionally bound via `x-model`.

# 4.Building User Interfaces with Alpine.js

Alpine.js is a lightweight JavaScript library that allows you to create reactive user interfaces with simple and intuitive syntax. Inspired by frameworks like Vue.js, Alpine.js provides a wide range of features to manipulate the DOM, manage events, and create dynamic components. However, Alpine.js stands out for its simplicity and ease of use, being specifically designed to add interactivity to existing or static applications without the need for complex builds or additional dependencies.

In this in-depth guide, we will explore how to **build user interfaces with Alpine.js**, focusing on **creating components**, **manipulating the DOM**, and **handling events**.

---

### 1. Creating Components with Alpine.js

#### 1.1. Defining Components in the Markup

Alpine.js allows you to define components directly in the HTML markup using the `x-data` directive. A component is essentially a portion of HTML code with its own state and behavior. Every time you use `x-data`, you are defining a new component.

Here's an example of a simple component:

```html
<div x-data="{ message: 'Hello World!' }">
    <h1 x-text="message"></h1>
</div>
```

In this example:

- The component has a local state defined by `x-data`, which contains the `message` property.

- The content of the `<h1>` element is dynamically populated using `x-text`, which replaces the content with the value of `message`.

#### 1.2. Composing Components

Components in Alpine.js can be nested inside one another, creating component hierarchies. This approach allows for modular and reusable user interfaces.

Here's an example of component composition:

```html
```

```
<div x-data="{ count: 0 }">
    <button @click="count++">Increase</button>
    <p x-text="count"></p>


    <!-- Subcomponent -->
    <div x-data="{ message: 'Hello from the subcomponent!' }">
        <p x-text="message"></p>
    </div>
</div>
```

In this case, we have two separate components. The main component contains a counter, while the subcomponent has its own state with the `message` variable. Notice that both components have isolated data since each use of `x-data` creates a new data context.

#### 1.3. Methods in Components

Alpine.js allows you to define methods directly within components. Methods are JavaScript functions that can be invoked in response to events or as part of the component's logic.

Here's how you define and use methods in Alpine.js:

```html
<div x-data="{ count: 0, increment() { this.count++ } }">
    <button @click="increment">Increase</button>
    <p x-text="count"></p>
</div>
```

- In addition to the `count` variable, we've defined a method called `increment`, which increases the counter. This method is executed when the button is clicked, thanks to the `@click` directive.

#### 1.4. Reusable Components with Templates

Alpine.js supports the use of HTML templates to create reusable components. A template defines a block of markup that can be reused multiple times within the same application.

Here's an example of using templates to create a reusable component:

```html
<template id="card-template">
    <div class="border p-4" x-data="{ title: 'Default Title' }">
```

```
    <h2 x-text="title"></h2>
    <slot></slot> <!-- For inserting dynamic content -->
  </div>
</template>

<div x-data>
  <template x-if="true">
    <div x-data="{ title: 'Custom Card' }">
      <h2 x-text="title"></h2>
    </div>
  </template>
</div>
```

In this example, we've defined a template called "card-template" that can be used as a base for multiple "cards" with customized titles.

---

### 2. Manipulating the DOM with Alpine.js

One of Alpine.js's key features is its ability to dynamically and reactively manipulate the DOM without the need for complex libraries or methods.

#### 2.1. Conditional Display: `x-show` and `x-if`

Alpine.js provides two main directives for managing the conditional display of elements: `x-show` and `x-if`.

- **`x-show`**: Controls the visibility of an element by hiding or showing it using `display: none` while keeping it in the DOM.

```html
<div x-data="{ visible: false }">
    <button @click="visible = ! visible">Toggle Visibility</button>
    <p x-show="visible">This paragraph is visible.</p>
</div>
```

- **`x-if`**: Unlike `x-show`, `x-if` completely removes the element from the DOM when the condition is false.

```html
<div x-data="{ isVisible: true }">
    <button @click="isVisible = ! isVisible">Toggle Visibility</button>
    <p x-if="isVisible">This paragraph only exists when visible.</p>
</div>
```

```

#### 2.2. Loops: `x-for`

Alpine.js allows you to create loops directly in the markup using the `x-for` directive. This is particularly useful for iterating over arrays or objects and generating elements dynamically.

```html
<div x-data="{ items: ['Apple', 'Banana', 'Orange'] }">

    <ul>

        <li x-for="item in items" x-text="item"></li>

    </ul>

</div>
```

In this example, `x-for` is used to iterate over
```

an array of fruits and display them in a `<ul>` list.

#### 2.3. Dynamic Attributes: `x-bind`

The `x-bind` directive allows you to dynamically bind HTML attribute values to component data. This can be used to modify classes, styles, custom attributes, and more.

Here's an example of using `x-bind` to manage dynamic classes and attributes:

```html
<div x-data="{ isActive: true }">
    <button x-bind:class="{ 'bg-blue-500': isActive, 'bg-gray-500': !isActive }">Toggle Classes</button>
</div>
```

In this example, the button's class changes dynamically based on the value of `isActive`. If `isActive` is true, the button will have the class `bg-blue-500`, otherwise `bg-gray-500`.

#### 2.4. Manipulating the DOM with `x-html`

Alpine.js provides the `x-html` directive to insert dynamic HTML code inside an element. This is useful when you want to insert HTML markup dynamically instead of simple text strings.

Here's an example of using `x-html`:

```html
<div x-data="{ content: '<strong>Bold Text</strong>' }">
    <div x-html="content"></div>
```

```
</div>
```

In this example, the HTML content is interpreted and inserted inside the `div`, displaying the text in bold.

#### 2.5. Dynamic Updates with `x-effect`

The `x-effect` directive allows you to execute side effects whenever data changes. This is particularly useful for updates or manipulations that are not immediately tied to events.

```html
<div x-data="{ value: 0 }">
    <input type="range" min="0" max="100" x-model="value">
    <div x-effect="console.log('Value changed:', value)"></div>
```

</div>

```

In this example, every time the value of the range slider changes, the `x-effect` effect is executed, printing the new value to the console.

---

### 3. Event Handling

Alpine.js simplifies event handling through its directives. Using the `@event` syntax, you can easily bind event handlers to HTML elements.

#### 3.1. Basic Events: `@click`, `@input`, `@mouseover`
```

The `@click` directive is one of the most commonly used in Alpine.js to bind functions to click events.

```html
<div x-data="{ count: 0 }">
    <button @click="count++">Increase</button>
    <p>You clicked <span x-text="count"></span> times.</p>
</div>
```

In this example, every time the button is clicked, the value of `count` is incremented and displayed in the paragraph.

In addition to `@click`, Alpine.js supports many other events such as `@input`, `@mouseover`, `@keydown`, etc.

```html
<div x-data="{ inputValue: '' }">
  <input type="text" @input="inputValue = $event.target.value" placeholder="Type something">
  <p x-text="inputValue"></p>
</div>
```

In this case, the `@input` event captures the user-typed value and stores it in `inputValue`.

#### 3.2. Event Modifiers

Alpine.js offers modifiers that can be used with events to handle more specific scenarios, such as running an event only once or preventing the default browser behavior.

Examples of event modifiers:

- **`.prevent`**: Prevents the default action of the event.

```html
<form @submit.prevent="alert('Submission prevented')">
    <button type="submit">Submit</button>
</form>
```

- **`.once`**: Executes the event only once.

```html
<button @click.once="alert('This will only run once')">Click Me</button>
```

- **`.debounce`**: Introduces a delay before

executing the event, useful for avoiding multiple unwanted executions.

```
```

html

```
<input type="text" @input.debounce.500="console.log('Input after 500ms pause')">
```

#### 3.3. Custom Events

Alpine.js allows you to trigger custom events and listen for them using the `x-on` directive. This is useful for communication between different components or for handling custom events within the application.

Here's an example of using custom events:

```html
<div x-data="{ sendEvent() { this.$dispatch('custom-event', { message: 'Event triggered!' }) } }">
    <button @click="sendEvent">Trigger Event</button>
</div>


<div x-data @custom-event.window="console.log($event.detail.message)">
    <!-- The custom event is listened to here -->
    <p>Check the console for the custom event message.</p>
</div>
```

In this case, we use the `$dispatch` method to trigger a custom event called `custom-event`. The second component listens for this event and prints the message to the console.

# 5. Alpine.js Directives

Alpine.js is a lightweight and powerful JavaScript library that allows you to add interactivity to web applications through the use of **directives**. The directives in Alpine.js are similar to those in other JavaScript frameworks like Vue.js and Angular, offering a declarative syntax for manipulating the DOM in a simple and direct way. This guide will explore the main Alpine.js directives, providing practical examples for each, and will include a final section on how to create custom directives.

---

### 1. Introduction to Alpine.js Directives

**Directives** in Alpine.js are special attributes that you can add to HTML elements to manage interactive behaviors. Directives allow you to associate variables, methods, and flow control logic directly with the markup. This clean and simple syntax makes Alpine.js easy to integrate into existing projects without the complexity of heavier frameworks.

Alpine.js directives are prefixed with `x-` (e.g., `x-data`, `x-show`, `x-bind`). This prefix helps distinguish Alpine directives from other HTML and CSS attributes, making it easier to integrate Alpine.js into any HTML project.

Here are some characteristics of Alpine.js directives:

- **Immediate reactivity**: Whenever data changes, the directives applied to the DOM automatically update.

- **Declarative**: There's no need to write imperative JavaScript code to update DOM elements. The directives handle this automatically.

- **Modular**: Each directive works independently, but they can be combined to create complex user interfaces.

Let's now explore the main Alpine.js directives and their use cases.

---

### 2. Main Alpine.js Directives

#### 2.1. `x-data`: Defining the Component

The `x-data` directive is the heart of Alpine.js, and it defines a component and its local state. Every time you use `x-data`, a context is created where Alpine.js manages the data and updates.

Example usage:

```html
```

```
<div x-data="{ message: 'Hello, Alpine!' }">
    <p x-text="message"></p>
</div>
```

In this example, `x-data` defines an object with a `message` property. The `x-text` directive, which we'll cover in detail later, updates the paragraph's text with the value of `message`.

#### 2.2. `x-show`: Conditional Display

The `x-show` directive is used to show or hide DOM elements based on a condition. It's similar to the CSS property `display: none`, but more efficient, as Alpine.js intelligently manages the DOM, keeping hidden elements in the DOM to avoid re-rendering.

Example usage:

```html
<div x-data="{ isVisible: false }">
    <button @click="isVisible = !isVisible">Toggle Visibility</button>
    <p x-show="isVisible">This text is only visible when isVisible is true.</p>
</div>
```

In this case, the paragraph will be shown or hidden based on the value of the `isVisible` property.

#### 2.3. `x-bind`: Dynamic Attribute Binding

`x-bind` allows dynamic binding of HTML attribute values to data objects managed by Alpine.js. This directive is powerful, enabling you to bind not only attributes like `class` or `style` but also any custom HTML attributes.

Example of `x-bind` usage:

```html
<div x-data="{ isActive: false }">
    <button @click="isActive = !isActive"
        x-bind:class="{ 'bg-blue-500': isActive, 'bg-gray-500': !isActive }">
        Toggle Classes
    </button>
</div>
```

Here, the button dynamically changes its class depending on the value of `isActive`. If `isActive` is true, the button will have the `bg-blue-500` class; otherwise, it will have `bg-gray-500`.

#### 2.4. `x-text`: Inserting Dynamic Text

`x-text` is used to insert text into an HTML element. It replaces the element's HTML content with the provided value.

Example usage:

```html
<div x-data="{ message: 'Hello World!' }">
   <p x-text="message"></p>
</div>
```

In this case, the `x-text` directive will replace the paragraph's content with the text defined in the `message` property.

#### 2.5. `x-html`: Inserting Dynamic HTML

Similar to `x-text`, but the difference is that `x-html` allows dynamic HTML content to be inserted into an element. This directive is useful when you need to insert dynamically generated HTML code.

Example usage:

```html
<div x-data="{ content: '<strong>Bold Text</strong>' }">
    <div x-html="content"></div>
</div>
```

Here, the HTML content is interpreted and inserted into the `div`, displaying the text in bold.

#### 2.6. `x-model`: Two-Way Data Binding

The `x-model` directive enables two-way data binding between DOM elements, such as input fields, and data managed by Alpine.js. Whenever the user modifies the input field, the associated data is automatically updated, and vice versa.

Example usage:

```html
<div x-data="{ message: 'Alpine.js' }">
    <input type="text" x-model="message">
    <p x-text="message"></p>
</div>
```

In this case, the input's value and the paragraph's text are linked in a two-way binding via `x-model`. Every time the input value changes, the paragraph updates with the new value, and vice versa.

#### 2.7. `x-for`: List Iteration

`x-for` allows you to iterate over arrays or objects and dynamically generate repeated HTML elements. It's similar to loops in other libraries, like `v-for` in Vue.js or `ng-repeat` in Angular.

Example usage:

```html
<div x-data="{ items: ['Apple', 'Banana', 'Orange'] }">
    <ul>
        <li x-for="item in items" x-text="item"></li>
    </ul>
```

        </div>
```

In this example, `x-for` loops over an array of fruits and generates a `<li>` for each item.

#### 2.8. `x-on`: Event Handling

Alpine.js simplifies event handling through the `x-on` directive, which can be shortened using the `@` syntax. This directive captures events like clicks, input changes, focus, and many others, linking them to methods or modifiers.

Example usage:

```html
<div x-data="{ count: 0 }">
    <button @click="count+

+"">Increment</button>

    <p x-text="count""></p>
</div>
```

In this example, every time the button is clicked, the `count` value is incremented and displayed in the paragraph.

#### 2.9. `x-effect`: Executing Side Effects

The `x-effect` directive allows you to execute side effects whenever data changes. This is useful for logic that isn't directly tied to specific events but needs to react to changes in the component's state.

Example usage:

```html

```
<div x-data="{ value: 0 }">
    <input type="range" min="0" max="100" x-model="value">
    <div x-effect="console.log('Value changed:', value)"></div>
</div>
```

In this example, every time the value of the range input changes, the `x-effect` runs and logs the new value to the console.

#### 2.10. `x-transition`: CSS Transitions

Alpine.js supports animated CSS transitions using the `x-transition` directive. This directive is useful when you want to animate the entrance or exit of an element from the page, such as animating a modal window.

Example usage:

```html
<div x-data="{ showModal: false }">
    <button @click="showModal = true">Show Modal</button>

    <div x-show="showModal" x-transition>
        <div class="modal">
            <p>This is an animated modal window!</p>
            <button @click="showModal = false">Close</button>
        </div>
    </div>
</div>
```

In this example, the modal window will appear and disappear with a smooth transition when the value of `showModal` changes.

---

### 3. Using Custom Directives

Alpine.js also allows you to define custom directives, extending its core functionality. Custom directives are useful when you want to reuse specific logic across multiple components or simplify DOM management.

To create a custom directive, Alpine.js provides the `Alpine.directive` function. Here's an example of a custom directive that dynamically changes an element's background color:

```javascript
Alpine.directive('color', (el, { expression },
{ evaluate }) => {

    el.style.backgroundColor =
```

```
evaluate(expression);
});
```

This directive can be used in the DOM as follows:

```html
<div x-data="{ color: 'lightblue' }">
    <div x-color="color">This div has a dynamic background color.</div>
</div>
```

In this example, the custom `x-color` directive applies a dynamic background color to the element based on the value of

the `color` variable.

---

Alpine.js directives are an essential part of building interactive and reactive web applications. They simplify state management, DOM manipulation, and event handling with a declarative syntax. By mastering key directives such as `x-show`, `x-bind`, `x-model`, and others, developers can create dynamic and responsive user interfaces effortlessly. Additionally, the ability to create custom directives allows for further flexibility, enabling developers to extend Alpine.js for specific needs, making it a versatile tool for any web project.

Understanding and combining these core directives opens up opportunities for building complex applications while keeping the code simple, readable, and maintainable.

# 6.Managing Complex States in Alpine.js

One of the most significant aspects of Alpine.js is its ability to manage state declaratively and reactively using the `x-data` directive. This guide will explore how to manage complex states in Alpine.js, with a particular focus on using `x-data` for state management, working with objects and arrays, and how to effectively reset and modify state.

---

### 1. Using `x-data` for State Management

The `x-data` directive in Alpine.js is used to define and manage a component's state. Every time `x-data` is used, a reactive data context is created within the DOM element, which can include variables, methods, and any other necessary logic.

#### 1.1. Defining Basic State

The simplest way to use `x-data` is to define a basic state, which is a JavaScript object that contains the variables and methods needed for your user interface.

Example of using `x-data` to manage a counter:

```html
<div x-data="{ count: 0 }">
    <button @click="count++">Increment</button>
    <p>Counter: <span x-text="count"></span></p>
</div>
```

In this example, `x-data` defines an object

with a `count` property initialized to 0. When the user clicks the button, the `count` value is incremented and displayed in the paragraph.

#### 1.2. Managing State with Methods

You can also define methods within the `x-data` object to handle more complex logic. These methods can be used to update the state or perform other operations.

Example of using methods to manage a counter with reset:

```html
<div x-data="{
    count: 0,
    increment() { this.count++ },
    reset() { this.count = 0 }
}">
```

```
    <button @click="increment">Increment</button>
    <button @click="reset">Reset</button>
    <p>Counter: <span x-text="count"></span></p>
</div>
```

In this example, besides the `count` property, we have two methods: `increment` and `reset`. `increment` increases the counter by 1, while `reset` resets it to 0.

#### 1.3. Using `x-data` with Initialization Functions

Sometimes it's useful to initialize the state using a function. This is especially helpful when the initial state is complex or needs to be calculated dynamically.

Example of using an initialization function:

```html
<div x-data="initData()">
   <button @click="increment">Increment</button>
   <button @click="reset">Reset</button>
   <p>Counter: <span x-text="count"></span></p>
</div>

<script>
function initData() {
   return {
      count: 0,
      increment() { this.count++ },
      reset() { this.count = 0 }
   }
}
```

```
</script>
```

In this example, `x-data` is initialized with the `initData` function, which returns an object containing the state and methods.

---

### 2. Working with Objects and Arrays

Alpine.js handles objects and arrays in a very similar way to plain JavaScript, but with the added benefit of automatic reactivity. This allows you to manage complex and structured states easily.

#### 2.1. Managing Objects

Objects can be used to organize state in a

more structured way. You can access and modify object properties directly in your Alpine.js components.

Example of using objects to manage a user profile:

```html
<div x-data="{ user: { name: 'Mario', age: 30 } }">

    <input type="text" x-model="user.name" placeholder="Name">

    <input type="number" x-model="user.age" placeholder="Age">

    <p>Name: <span x-text="user.name"></span></p>

    <p>Age: <span x-text="user.age"></span></p>

</div>
```

In this example, the state is an object `user` containing `name` and `age`. The inputs are linked to the object's properties using `x-model`, and the values are dynamically displayed.

#### 2.2. Managing Arrays

Arrays can be used to manage lists of data. Alpine.js provides directives like `x-for` to iterate over arrays and dynamically generate content.

Example of using arrays to manage a list of items:

```html
<div x-data="{ items: ['Apple', 'Banana', 'Orange'] }">
    <ul>
        <li x-for="item in items" x-
```

```
text="item"></li>
    </ul>
    <input type="text" x-model="newItem" placeholder="New item">
    <button @click="items.push(newItem); newItem = ''">Add</button>
</div>
```

In this example, the `items` array is used to generate a `<ul>` list. An input and a button allow the user to add new items to the array.

#### 2.3. Manipulating Objects and Arrays

When working with objects and arrays, you may need to perform operations like updating properties or adding/removing elements. Alpine.js handles these operations reactively, automatically updating the DOM.

Example of manipulating an array of objects:

```html
<div x-data="{
    todos: [
        { text: 'Buy milk', done: false },
        { text: 'Do groceries', done: true }
    ],
    toggleDone(todo) {
        todo.done = !todo.done;
    }
}">
    <ul>
        <li x-for="todo in todos">
            <input type="checkbox" x-model="todo.done">
            <span x-text="todo.text" :class="{ 'line-through': todo.done }"></span>
            <button
```

```
            @click="toggleDone(todo)">Toggle Done</button>
        </li>
      </ul>
    </div>
```

In this example, each item in the `todos` list is an object with a `done` property. The `toggleDone` method changes the `done` state, and the CSS updates based on its value.

---

### 3. Resetting and Modifying State

Alpine.js offers simple ways to reset and modify state. It's important to know how to manipulate the state effectively to ensure your user interface responds correctly to user actions.

#### 3.1. Resetting State

To reset the state, you can simply assign new values to the properties in your `x-data` object. You can do this directly inside a method or in response to an event.

Example of resetting the counter and array:

```html
<div x-data="{
    count: 0,
    items: ['Apple', 'Banana', 'Orange'],
    reset() {
        this.count = 0;
        this.items = ['Apple', 'Banana', 'Orange'];
    }
}">
    <button @click="count+
```

```
+">Increment</button>
    <button @click="reset">Reset</button>
    <p>Counter: <span x-text="count"></span></p>

    <ul>
        <li x-for="item in items" x-text="item"></li>
    </ul>
    <button @click="reset">Reset List</button>
</div>
```

In this example, the `reset` method resets both the counter and the item list to their initial values. You can adapt this logic to reset any part of the state.

#### 3.2. Modifying State

Modifying state in Alpine.js is simple and direct. You can update properties directly or use methods to handle more complex changes.

Example of modifying user state:

```html
<div x-data="{
  user: { name: 'Mario', age: 30 },
  updateName(event) {
    this.user.name = event.target.value;
  },
  updateAge(event) {
    this.user.age = parseInt(event.target.value, 10);
  }
}">
  <input type="text" x-model="user.name"
```

```
    @input="updateName" placeholder="Name">
    <input type="number" x-model="user.age" @input="updateAge" placeholder="Age">
    <p>Name: <span x-text="user.name"></span></p>
    <p>Age: <span x-text="user.age"></span></p>
</div>
```

In this example, the `updateName` and `updateAge` methods update the user's name and age based on user input.

#### 3.3. Using Computed Properties

Alpine.js doesn't have an explicit concept of computed properties like Vue.js, but you can easily create computed properties within `x-data` using methods and getters.

Example of a computed property for a full name:

```html
<div x-data="{
    firstName: 'Mario',
    lastName: 'Rossi',
    get fullName() {
        return this.firstName + ' ' + this.lastName;
    }
}">
    <p>Full Name: <span x-text="fullName"></span></p>
    <input type="text" x-model="firstName" placeholder="First Name">
    <input type="text" x-model="lastName" placeholder="Last Name">
</div>
```

In this example, the `fullName` property is computed by concatenating `firstName` and `lastName`. Whenever one of the values changes, `fullName` is automatically updated.

---

Managing complex states in Alpine.js is powerful and flexible, allowing you to create dynamic, reactive user interfaces with simple declarative code. Using `x-data`, you can define and manage your components' state clearly and structurally. Working with objects and arrays allows you to handle more complex data, while reset and modification operations give you the control needed to manage user interactions.

# 7. Animations and Transitions in Alpine.js

Alpine.js is a lightweight JavaScript library designed to add interactivity to your web pages with a simple and declarative syntax. One of the most powerful features of Alpine.js is its ability to handle animations and transitions, enhancing the user experience and making interactions smoother and more engaging. In this guide, we will explore how to add animations to interactions using Alpine.js and how to use CSS classes to manage animations. We will provide detailed examples to help you implement sophisticated visual effects in your web applications.

---

### 1. Adding Animations to Interactions

Animations can transform the user experience by making interactions with your application more engaging. Alpine.js offers a simple syntax for adding animations to interactions using the `x-transition` directives. These directives allow you to apply animations when elements enter or leave the DOM and can be customized to achieve various effects.

#### 1.1. Introduction to `x-transition`

The `x-transition` directive is used to manage element transition animations. It can be applied to any element that uses `x-show` to control visibility and allows you to define animations for the element's entry and exit states.

##### 1.1.1. Entry and Exit Transitions

Example of a simple entry and exit transition:

```html
<div x-data="{ show: false }">
```

```html
<button @click="show = !show">Show/Hide</button>

<div x-show="show"
     x-transition:enter="transition ease-out duration-300"
     x-transition:enter-start="opacity-0 transform scale-90"
     x-transition:enter-end="opacity-100 transform scale-100"
     x-transition:leave="transition ease-in duration-300"
     x-transition:leave-start="opacity-100 transform scale-100"
     x-transition:leave-end="opacity-0 transform scale-90"
     class="p-4 bg-blue-500 text-white">
    This element appears and disappears with a fade and zoom transition.
</div>
</div>
```

```

In this example:

- `x-show` controls the element's visibility.

- `x-transition:enter` and `x-transition:leave` define the CSS classes for entry and exit transitions.

- `x-transition:enter-start`, `x-transition:enter-end`, `x-transition:leave-start`, and `x-transition:leave-end` define the initial and final states of the transitions.

##### 1.1.2. State Change Transition

Transitions can also be applied to state changes:

```html
<div x-data="{ open: false }">
    <button @click="open = !

```html
open">Open/Close</button>

<div x-show="open"
    x-transition:enter="transition transform ease-out duration-500"
    x-transition:enter-start="opacity-0 transform translate-y-10"
    x-transition:enter-end="opacity-100 transform translate-y-0"
    x-transition:leave="transition transform ease-in duration-500"
    x-transition:leave-start="opacity-100 transform translate-y-0"
    x-transition:leave-end="opacity-0 transform translate-y-10"
    class="p-4 bg-green-500 text-white">
    This element slides up and down during open and close transitions.
</div>
</div>
```

```

In this example, the element slides vertically during entry and exit transitions.

#### 1.2. Customizing Transitions

Transitions can be further customized by combining the `x-transition` directives with CSS classes for more complex effects.

##### 1.2.1. Slide Transition Effect

Example of a horizontal slide transition:

```html
<style>
/* Add these classes to your CSS */
.slide-enter {

```css
    transform: translateX(-100%);
    opacity: 0;
}
.slide-enter-active {
    transition: transform 0.5s ease, opacity 0.5s ease;
    transform: translateX(0);
    opacity: 1;
}
.slide-leave {
    transform: translateX(0);
    opacity: 1;
}
.slide-leave-active {
    transition: transform 0.5s ease, opacity 0.5s ease;
    transform: translateX(100%);
    opacity: 0;
}
```

```
</style>

<div x-data="{ show: false }">
    <button @click="show = !show">Show/Hide</button>

    <div x-show="show"
        x-transition:enter="slide-enter"
        x-transition:enter-active="slide-enter-active"
        x-transition:leave="slide-leave"
        x-transition:leave-active="slide-leave-active"
        class="p-4 bg-purple-500 text-white">
        This element slides from left to right during transitions.
    </div>
</div>
```

In this example, we defined CSS classes to manage the horizontal sliding effect.

##### 1.2.2. Zoom Animation Transition

Example of zoom in and out animation:

```html
<style>
@keyframes zoom-in {
    from {
        transform: scale(0.5);
        opacity: 0;
    }
    to {
        transform: scale(1);
        opacity: 1;
    }
```

```css
}
@keyframes zoom-out {
  from {
    transform: scale(1);
    opacity: 1;
  }
  to {
    transform: scale(0.5);
    opacity: 0;
  }
}
.zoom-in-enter {
  animation: zoom-in 0.5s forwards;
}
.zoom-out-leave {
  animation: zoom-out 0.5s forwards;
}
</style>
```

```html
<div x-data="{ show: false }">
    <button @click="show = !show">Show/Hide</button>

    <div x-show="show"
        x-transition:enter="zoom-in-enter"
        x-transition:leave="zoom-out-leave"
        class="p-4 bg-teal-500 text-white">
        This element zooms in and out during transitions.
    </div>
</div>
```

In this example, zoom animations are applied when the element enters or leaves the DOM.

---

### 2. Using CSS Classes for Animations

CSS animations offer detailed control over visual effects and can be easily integrated into Alpine.js. CSS classes can be used to apply predefined or custom animations to DOM elements.

#### 2.1. Defining CSS Animations

CSS animations are defined using the `@keyframes` rules, which specify the animation's progression over time. CSS classes apply these animations to elements.

##### 2.1.1. Defining a Pulse Animation

Example of a pulse animation:

```html
<style>
@keyframes pulse {
  0% {
    transform: scale(1);
    opacity: 1;
  }
  50% {
    transform: scale(1.1);
    opacity: 0.8;
  }
  100% {
    transform: scale(1);
    opacity: 1;
  }
}
.pulse-animation {
  animation: pulse 2s infinite;
```

```
}
</style>

<div x-data="{ animate: false }">
  <button @click="animate = ! animate">Start/Stop Animation</button>

  <div :class="{ 'pulse-animation': animate }" class="p-4 bg-red-500 text-white">
    This element pulses when `animate` is true.
  </div>
</div>
```

In this example:

- The `@keyframes` rule defines the pulse animation.

- The `pulse-animation` CSS class applies the animation to the element.

- Alpine.js's `:class` directive applies or removes the class based on the value of the `animate` variable.

##### 2.1.2. Defining a Bounce Animation

Example of a bounce animation:

```html
<style>
@keyframes bounce {
  0%, 20%, 50%, 80%, 100% {
    transform: translateY(0);
  }
  40% {
    transform: translateY(-30px);
  }
  60% {
    transform: translateY(-15px);
```

```
    }
}
.bounce-animation {
    animation: bounce 1s;
}
</style>

<div x-data="{ bounce: false }">
    <button @click="bounce = ! bounce">Bounce</button>

    <div :class="{ 'bounce-animation': bounce }" class="p-4 bg-yellow-500 text-white">
        This element bounces when `bounce` is true.
    </div>
</div>
```

In this example:

- The `@keyframes` rule defines the bounce animation.

- The `bounce-animation` CSS class applies the animation to the element.

- Alpine.js's `:class` directive manages the class application based on the value of `bounce`.

#### 2.2. CSS Entry and Exit Animations

Entry and exit animations can be fully managed with CSS, combining `x-transition` with custom CSS classes.

##### 2.2.1. Entry Animation with Zoom Effect

Example of an entry animation with a zoom effect:

```html
<style>
@keyframes zoom-in {
  from {
    transform: scale(0.5);
    opacity: 0;
  }
  to {
    transform: scale(1);
    opacity: 1;
  }
}
@keyframes zoom-out {
  from {
    transform: scale(1);
    opacity: 1;
  }
```

```css
  to {
    transform: scale(0.5);
    opacity: 0;
  }
}
.zoom-in-enter {
  animation: zoom-in 0.5s forwards;
}
.zoom-out-leave {
  animation: zoom-out 0.5s forwards;
}
</style>
```

```html
<div x-data="{ show: false }">
  <button @click="show = !show">Show/Hide</button>

  <div x-show="show"
```

    x-transition:enter="zoom-in-enter"
    x-transition:leave="zoom-out-leave"
    class="p-4 bg-teal-500 text-white">
    This element zooms in and out during transitions.
  </div>
</div>
```

In this example, zoom animations are applied when the element enters or leaves the DOM.
```

# 8.Integration with Other Technologies and Practical Examples in Alpine.js

Alpine.js is a lightweight JavaScript library that integrates well with a variety of modern technologies and tools. In this document, we will explore how to integrate Alpine.js with Laravel, interact with external APIs, and combine it with Tailwind CSS. We will also provide practical examples such as creating a dropdown menu, an interactive contact form, and an image gallery. Finally, we will discuss best practices for structuring code, optimizing performance, and debugging in Alpine.js.

---

## Integration with Other Technologies

### Using Alpine.js with Laravel

Laravel is a popular PHP framework for web

development and integrates seamlessly with Alpine.js. Alpine.js can be used in Laravel to add interactivity to your pages without writing complex JavaScript code.

#### 1.1. Setting Up Alpine.js in a Laravel Project

To integrate Alpine.js into a Laravel project, you can follow these steps:

##### 1.1.1. Installation via npm

If you are using Laravel Mix for asset management, you can install Alpine.js via npm:

```bash
npm install alpinejs
```

Then, import Alpine.js in your `resources/js/app.js` file:

```javascript
import Alpine from 'alpinejs';

window.Alpine = Alpine;

Alpine.start();
```

Don't forget to compile your assets with Laravel Mix:

```bash
npm run dev
```

##### 1.1.2. Including Alpine.js via CDN

Alternatively, you can include Alpine.js directly in your Blade layout using a CDN. Add the following code to your Blade file, usually `resources/views/layouts/app.blade.php`:

```html
<!DOCTYPE html>
<html lang="en">
<head>
    <meta charset="UTF-8">
    <meta name="viewport" content="width=device-width, initial-scale=1.0">
    <title>Document</title>
    <!-- Include Alpine.js via CDN -->
    <script src="https://cdn.jsdelivr.net/npm/alpinejs@3.12.2/dist/cdn.min.js" defer></script>
    <!-- Include Tailwind CSS (optional) -->
```

```
    <link href="https://cdn.jsdelivr.net/npm/tailwindcss@2.2.19/dist/tailwind.min.css" rel="stylesheet">
</head>
<body>
    @yield('content')
</body>
</html>
```

This way, Alpine.js will be available for all your Laravel pages without further configuration.

#### 1.2. Using Alpine.js with Blade Templates

Laravel Blade is a powerful templating engine that allows you to generate dynamic HTML. You can use Alpine.js directly within your Blade files to add interactivity.

Example of using Alpine.js in a Blade template:

```html
<!-- resources/views/welcome.blade.php -->
@extends('layouts.app')

@section('content')
<div x-data="{ open: false }">
    <button @click="open = !open" class="bg-blue-500 text-white p-2 rounded">
        Toggle Menu
    </button>

    <div x-show="open" class="mt-2 bg-gray-200 p-4 rounded">
        This menu is shown or hidden with Alpine.js.
```

```
        </div>
    </div>
@endsection
```

In this example, a menu is shown or hidden by clicking a button, using the `x-show` directive of Alpine.js.

### Interacting with External APIs

Alpine.js is perfect for interacting with external APIs thanks to its simplicity and reactivity. You can make API requests and handle data directly within your Alpine.js components.

#### 2.1. Example of Interacting with an API

Suppose you want to fetch data from an API

and display it to the user. Here's an example of how to do this:

```html
<div x-data="fetchData()">
  <button @click="loadData" class="bg-blue-500 text-white p-2 rounded">
    Load Data
  </button>

  <div x-show="loading" class="mt-2">Loading...</div>

  <ul x-show="!loading && data.length > 0" class="mt-2">
    <template x-for="item in data" :key="item.id">
      <li class="border p-2 mb-2">{{ item.name }}</li>
    </template>
```

```html
    </ul>
```

```html
    <div x-show="!loading && data.length === 0" class="mt-2">No data available.</div>
</div>
```

```html
<script>
```
```javascript
function fetchData() {
    return {
        data: [],
        loading: false,
        async loadData() {
            this.loading = true;
            try {
                const response = await fetch('https://api.example.com/items');
                this.data = await response.json();
            } catch (error) {
```

```
            console.error('Error loading data:', error);
        } finally {
            this.loading = false;
        }
      }
   }
}
</script>
```

In this example:

- `fetchData()` is a function that returns an Alpine.js object with API data, a loading state, and a function to load the data.

- `loadData` is an asynchronous function that fetches data from the API and updates the component's state.

### Integrating with Tailwind CSS

Tailwind CSS is a CSS framework that allows you to build modern, responsive user interfaces using utility classes. Alpine.js and Tailwind CSS integrate well, allowing you to build interactive and styled interfaces efficiently.

#### 3.1. Installing Tailwind CSS

If you haven't already installed Tailwind CSS in your Laravel project, you can do so with npm:

```bash
npm install tailwindcss
```

Then, create a Tailwind CSS configuration file:

```bash
npx tailwindcss init
```

Configure Tailwind CSS in your `resources/css/app.css` file:

```css
@tailwind base;
@tailwind components;
@tailwind utilities;
```

Compile your CSS:

```bash
npm run dev
```

#### 3.2. Example of Integrating Alpine.js and Tailwind CSS

Here's an example of combining Alpine.js and Tailwind CSS to build a dropdown menu:

```html
<div x-data="{ open: false }" class="relative inline-block text-left">
    <button @click="open = !open" class="bg-blue-500 text-white px-4 py-2 rounded">
        Menu
    </button>

    <div x-show="open" @click.away="open = false" class="absolute right-0 mt-2 w-48 bg-white border border-gray-300 rounded shadow-lg z-10">
        <a href="#" class="block px-4 py-2 text-gray-700 hover:bg-gray--100">Option 1</a>
        <a href="#" class="block px-4 py-2 text-
```

gray-700 hover:bg-gray-100">Option 2</a>

    <a href="#" class="block px-4 py-2 text-gray-700 hover:bg-gray-100">Option 3</a>

  </div>

</div>
```

In this example:

- The button shows or hides the dropdown menu.

- `x-show` handles the visibility of the menu.

- The `absolute` class and other Tailwind CSS classes manage the position and styling of the menu.

---

## Practical Examples
```

### Creating a Dropdown Menu

The dropdown menu is a common component in user interfaces. Using Alpine.js and Tailwind CSS, you can create an elegant and interactive dropdown menu.

Here's an example of a dropdown menu:

```html
<div x-data="{ open: false }" class="relative inline-block text-left">

    <button @click="open = !open" class="bg-blue-500 text-white px-4 py-2 rounded">

        Menu

    </button>


    <div x-show="open" @click.away="open = false" class="absolute right-0 mt-2 w-48 bg-white border border-gray-300 rounded shadow-lg z-10">
```

```html
    <a href="#" class="block px-4 py-2 text-gray-700 hover:bg-gray-100">Option 1</a>
    <a href="#" class="block px-4 py-2 text-gray-700 hover:bg-gray-100">Option 2</a>
    <a href="#" class="block px-4 py-2 text-gray-700 hover:bg-gray-100">Option 3</a>
  </div>
</div>
```

### Building an Interactive Contact Form

An interactive contact form can use Alpine.js to manage validation and display error messages.

Here's an example of a contact form:

```html
<div x-data="contactForm()" class="max-w-lg mx-auto p-4">
```

```
<form @submit.prevent="submitForm"
class="space-y-4">

    <div>

        <label for="name" class="block text-
sm font-medium text-gray-
700">Name</label>

        <input type="text" id="name" x-
model="name" class="mt-1 block w-full
border border-gray-300 rounded-md shadow-
sm">

        <p x-show="errors.name" class="text-
red-500 text-xs mt-1" x-
text="errors.name"></p>

    </div>

    <div>

        <label for="email" class="block text-
sm font-medium text-gray-
700">Email</label>

        <input type="email" id="email" x-
model="email" class="mt-1 block w-full
border border-gray-300 rounded-md shadow-
sm">

            <p x-show="errors.email" class="text-
```

```html
red-500 text-xs mt-1" x-text="errors.email"></p>
    </div>
    <div>
        <label for="message" class="block text-sm font-medium text-gray-700">Message</label>
        <textarea id="message" x-model="message" rows="4" class="mt-1 block w-full border border-gray-300 rounded-md shadow-sm"></textarea>
        <p x-show="errors.message" class="text-red-500 text-xs mt-1" x-text="errors.message"></p>
    </div>
    <button type="submit" class="bg-blue-500 text-white px-4 py-2 rounded">Send</button>
    <p x-show="successMessage" class="text-green-500 mt-2" x-text="successMessage"></p>
```

```
    </form>
</div>


<script>
function contactForm() {
    return {
        name: '',
        email: '',
        message: '',
        errors: {},
        successMessage: '',
        async submitForm() {
            this.errors = {};
            this.successMessage = '';

            // Validation
            if (!this.name) this.errors.name = 'Name is required.';
```

```
    if (!this.email) this.errors.email = 'Email is required.';
    if (!this.message) this.errors.message = 'Message is required.';

    if (Object.keys(this.errors).length > 0) return;

    // Simulate form submission
    try {
      // Imagine this call sends the data to a server
      await new Promise(resolve => setTimeout(resolve, 1000));
      this.successMessage = 'Message sent successfully!';
      this.name = '';
      this.email = '';
      this.message = '';
    } catch (error) {
```

```
                    console.error('Error submitting the form:', error);
                }
            }
        }
    }
}
</script>
```

### Creating an Image Gallery

An image gallery can be built with Alpine.js to manage interaction and dynamic display of images.

Here's an example of an image gallery:

```html
<div x-data="{ currentIndex: 0, images:
```

['img1.jpg', 'img2.jpg', 'img3.jpg'] }" class="max-w-lg mx-auto">

  &lt;div class="relative"&gt;

    &lt;img :src="images[currentIndex]" class="w-full h-64 object-cover"&gt;

    &lt;button @click="currentIndex = (currentIndex - 1 + images.length) % images.length" class="absolute top-1/2 left-4 transform -translate-y-1/2 bg-black text-white p-2 rounded"&gt;←&lt;/button&gt;

    &lt;button @click="currentIndex = (currentIndex + 1) % images.length" class="absolute top-1/2 right-4 transform -translate-y-1/2 bg-black text-white p-2 rounded"&gt;→&lt;/button&gt;

  &lt;/div&gt;

  &lt;div class="mt-4 flex justify-center space-x-2"&gt;

    &lt;template x-for="(image, index) in images" :key="index"&gt;

      &lt;button @click="currentIndex = index" class="w-16 h-16"&gt;

        &lt;img :src="image" class="w-full h-

          full object-cover rounded">
        </button>
      </template>
    </div>
  </div>
```

---

## Best Practices

### Structuring Code

To keep code organized and maintainable, consider the following best practices:

1. **Modularity**: Create reusable and well-defined components for different parts of the user interface.
```

2. **Separation of Concerns**: Keep JavaScript logic separate from HTML markup when possible.

3. **Use Functions**: Utilize functions to handle state logic and interactions in Alpine.js.

### Performance Optimization

Alpine.js is designed to be lightweight, but it's still important to follow best practices to optimize performance:

1. **Minimize DOM**: Reduce DOM updates to improve reactivity.

2. **Use `x-data` Carefully**: Avoid creating too many nested `x-data` components that can impact performance.

3. **Debouncing and Throttling**: Use debouncing and throttling techniques for frequently occurring events (e.g., window resizing).

### Debugging in Alpine.js

Debugging Alpine.js can be done using browser developer tools and the following techniques:

1. **Console Logging**: Use `console.log` to view variable values and program flow.

2. **DevTools**: Use browser development tools to inspect elements and verify Alpine.js directives are applied correctly.

3. **Directive Verification**: Ensure Alpine.js directives are correctly applied and dependencies are satisfied.

# 9. Alpine.js Glossary

To fully understand how to use Alpine.js and make the most of it, it's helpful to know some of the key terms and concepts associated with this library. In this section, we will explore the main terms and directives of Alpine.js and provide a summary of the changelog, which will help you understand how and when new updates and improvements have been introduced.

---

## Directive References

Directives are the heart of Alpine.js, allowing you to add dynamic behavior to HTML elements with a simple syntax. Here is an overview of the main Alpine.js directives:

### 1. `x-data`

**Description**: The `x-data` directive is used to initialize reactive state within an element. It defines an Alpine.js component and specifies the data and functions available.

**Syntax**:

```html
<div x-data="{ count: 0 }">
    <p x-text="count"></p>
    <button @click="count++">Increment</button>
</div>
```

**Details**: In this example, `x-data` initializes an object with a `count` property and a method to increment it. The `<p>` element displays the value of `count`, and the button increments the value when clicked.

### 2. `x-show`

**Description**: The `x-show` directive controls the visibility of an element based on a boolean condition. Elements are shown or hidden without being removed from the DOM.

**Syntax**:

```html
<div x-data="{ open: false }">
    <button @click="open = ! open">Toggle</button>
    <div x-show="open">This is conditional text.</div>
</div>
```

**Details**: `x-show` shows or hides content based on the value of the `open` property. Elements are always present in the DOM, but their visibility changes.

### 3. `x-bind`

**Description**: The `x-bind` directive is used to bind HTML attributes to Alpine.js states. It allows you to dynamically bind values to element attributes.

**Syntax**:

```html
<div x-data="{ isActive: true }">
    <button :class="{ 'bg-blue-500': isActive, 'bg-gray-500': !isActive }" @click="isActive = !isActive">
        Toggle Class
    </button>
```

</div>
```

**Details**: In this example, `x-bind:class` (shortened as `:class`) changes the button's class based on the value of `isActive`.

### 4. `x-model`

**Description**: The `x-model` directive creates a two-way binding between an input and a state property, similar to Vue.js's `v-model`.

**Syntax**:

```html
<div x-data="{ message: '' }">
    <input x-model="message" placeholder="Type something...">

```
  <p x-text="message"></p>
</div>
```

**Details**: `x-model` binds the value of the input to the `message` property. Any change in the input updates the property and vice versa.

### 5. `x-on` / `@`

**Description**: The `x-on` directive (shortened as `@`) handles HTML element events, associating actions with state changes.

**Syntax**:

```html
<div x-data="{ count: 0 }">
  <button @click="count+
```

+"">Increment</button>

    <p x-text="count"></p>
</div>
```

**Details**: `@click` is a shorthand for `x-on:click`. It attaches an event handler to the button click to increment the `count` value.

### 6. `x-transition`

**Description**: The `x-transition` directive manages CSS transitions when elements are shown or hidden. It allows for smooth animations during visibility changes.

**Syntax**:

```html
<div x-data="{ show: false }">

```
<button @click="show = !show">Toggle</button>

<div x-show="show" x-transition:enter="transition ease-out duration-300" x-transition:leave="transition ease-in duration-200">
    This element has a transition.
</div>
</div>
```

**Details**: `x-transition` applies CSS classes during enter and leave transitions, enhancing the user experience with smooth animations.

### 7. `x-if`

**Description**: The `x-if` directive adds or removes elements from the DOM based on a boolean condition. It is similar to `x-show`, but removes the element from the DOM when the condition is false.

**Syntax**:

```html
<div x-data="{ show: false }">
   <button @click="show = ! show">Toggle</button>
   <template x-if="show">
      <div>This element is added or removed from the DOM.</div>
   </template>
</div>
```

**Details**: `x-if` uses a `<template>` element to manage adding and removing elements from the DOM, useful for managing performance in complex situations.

### 8. `x-for`

**Description**: The `x-for` directive is used to create lists of elements by iterating over arrays or objects. It works similarly to `for` loops in JavaScript.

**Syntax**:

```html
<div x-data="{ items: ['Item 1', 'Item 2', 'Item 3'] }">
    <ul>
        <template x-for="(item, index) in items" :key="index">
            <li x-text="item"></li>
        </template>
    </ul>
</div>
```

```

**Details**: `x-for` iterates over an `items` array, creating an `<li>` element for each item in the array.

### 9. `x-effect`

**Description**: The `x-effect` directive allows you to run a function every time a state changes, useful for executing side effects based on state changes.

**Syntax**:

```html
<div x-data="{ count: 0 }" x-effect="console.log('Count changed:', count)">

  <button @click="count++">Increment</button>

```html
<p x-text="count"></p>
</div>
```

**Details**: `x-effect` runs `console.log` every time the `count` value changes, allowing you to monitor or react to state changes.

### 10. `x-cloak`

**Description**: The `x-cloak` directive hides elements until Alpine.js is fully loaded and ready. This prevents a flash of unstyled content.

**Syntax**:

```html
<div x-data="{ open: false }" x-cloak>
```

```
    <button @click="open = !open">Toggle</button>
    <div x-show="open">This is initially hidden content.</div>
</div>


<style>
[x-cloak] { display: none; }
</style>
```

**Details**: `x-cloak` uses the CSS property `display: none` to hide the element until Alpine.js applies the logic and transitions.

# Index

1. Introduction to Alpine.js pg.4

2. Getting Started with Alpine.js 18

3. Fundamental Concepts of Alpine.js pg.37

4. Building User Interfaces with Alpine.js pg.52

5. Alpine.js Directives pg.72

6. Managing Complex States in Alpine.js pg.89

7. Animations and Transitions in Alpine.js pg.106

**8.Integration with Other Technologies and Practical Examples in Alpine.js pg.126**

**9.Alpine.js Glossary pg.151**

www.ingramcontent.com/pod-product-compliance
Lightning Source LLC
Chambersburg PA
CBHW052204220526
45471CB00004B/1803